Original title:
Echoes of Existence

Author: Liina Liblikas
ISBN HARDBACK: 978-1-80560-961-2
ISBN PAPERBACK: 978-1-80561-522-4

Silence of the Unseen

In shadows deep where whispers dwell,
The quiet speaks, a timeless spell.
Each breath a ghost, a muffled sound,
In silence vast, all truths are found.

Beyond the veil, where dreams collide,
The unseen world, where souls abide.
A tapestry of hearts entwined,
In silence soft, our peace we find.

Traces of Lives Lived

Footprints mark the sands of time,
Each step a story, rhythm and rhyme.
In laughter shared and tears we shed,
We paint the paths of those long dead.

Memories woven, threads of gold,
In every tale, our lives unfold.
The echoes of past, a sweet refrain,
Traces of love and lingering pain.

Harmonics of Worn Paths

Where traveler's feet have long since gone,
The path sings softly, a gentle song.
With every stone, each bend and flow,
The harmonies of life still glow.

Rustling leaves in the evening light,
Call forth the whispers of day and night.
In shadows cast by the setting sun,
The story of wanderers is spun.

The Essence of Fading Light

As daylight wanes and shadows creep,
The essence stirs from quiet sleep.
Colors dim and dreams take flight,
In the embrace of fading light.

Moments linger, a fleeting kiss,
In twilight's grasp, we find our bliss.
Each ray that wanes, a tale to tell,
In the hush of dusk, we bid farewell.

Remnants of a Faded Light

In twilight's hush, shadows dance,
Flickering flames in a lost romance.
Whispers linger on cool night's breath,
Hope entwined with the threads of death.

Memories fade like the stars at dawn,
Echoes of dreams now forlorn.
The past wraps tight with a velvet sigh,
Leaving hearts heavy as time drifts by.

Crimson skies paint a tale untold,
Of love that gathered, then turned to gold.
Each moment trapped in the amber glow,
A bittersweet warmth in shadows below.

But in the stillness, a spark may glow,
A flicker of life in the afterflow.
From ashes rise, a new path ignites,
As dawn awakens the remnants of night.

Ghosts in the Silence

In quiet corridors where shadows play,
Whispers cling to the light of day.
Footsteps echo in an empty hall,
Memories linger, they rise then fall.

Faces faded in the mist of time,
Carry secrets like an old rhyme.
Silent voices call out in fright,
To be heard within the shroud of night.

The weight of history hangs in the air,
Every sigh filled with longing and care.
Hushed confessions in the moon's pale glow,
Speak of tales only the lonely know.

Yet in the silence, a story swells,
Of loves once vibrant, now hidden spells.
Perhaps the ghosts dance in plain sight,
In the whispers of shadows that grace the night.

The Language of Lost Souls

In shadows deep, where memories drift,
Lost souls wander, seeking a gift.
Words unspoken in the hush of night,
Echo softly, a beacon of light.

Each sigh a message, a tale to impart,
Tangled emotions within every heart.
Questions linger like fog on the ground,
In silence, the answers are often found.

Fragments of laughter, a bittersweet strain,
Haunt the echoes of joy and pain.
Meeting in glances, they search and yearn,
For the language of love, destined to burn.

In the twilight where dreams intertwine,
They find solace in the unbroken line.
For even in darkness, hope's voice will rise,
Guiding the lost through the starlit skies.

Eclipsed Moments

Beneath the veil of a crescent moon,
Moments linger, yet end all too soon.
Fleeting shadows brush past our way,
In the dance of night, we silently sway.

The world holds its breath in the stillness,
Each heartbeat echoes with a thrillness.
Fragments of time caught in the gleam,
Rippling softly like a forgotten dream.

In the eclipse, secrets tethered tight,
Await their moment to break into light.
As destiny pauses in a lover's glance,
We rewrite fate in this daring dance.

Unraveling threads that tether the past,
In the warmth of the now, we find we last.
Eclipsed by love, we learn to ignite,
Painting the night with our softest light.

Notes from the Great Beyond

Whispers of stars in a velvet night,
Echoes of dreams beyond our sight.
Time drifts like clouds, soft and slow,
In silence, the secrets of ages flow.

Shadows dance with the lunar glow,
Memories hidden, like rivers below.
Hearts that linger, lost in the mist,
In the great beyond, there's magic we've missed.

Voices of ancients, gentle and kind,
Threads of the past forever entwined.
Stories of love, pain, and grace,
In the vast cosmos, we find our place.

Each twinkle a story, a life lived well,
In the fabric of time, our spirits dwell.
Connecting the dots in the great expanse,
A universe rich in our timeless dance.

So listen close to the night's soft song,
Feel the pulse of the earth and belong.
For in every heartbeat, the cosmos calls,
Notes from the great beyond encompass us all.

Half-Remembered Horizons

In the twilight where shadows play,
Half-remembered dreams drift away.
Fleeting moments lost in the haze,
We chase the echoes of brighter days.

A canvas splashed with colors bright,
Each stroke a whisper, a soft delight.
Yet clarity fades as time moves on,
Leaving us yearning for what is gone.

Horizons shift like the tide's embrace,
The sun dips low, a golden trace.
In the distance, hopes begin to fade,
Yet the heart holds tight to the dreams we made.

Fragments of laughter and tears reside,
In the corners where memories hide.
Each thought a treasure, a path untried,
Guiding us gently on life's long ride.

So we wander forth, though unsure and lost,
Navigating life's map at any cost.
For even in shadows, we find our way,
Toward half-remembered horizons, we sway.

Interlude of the Soul

In stillness, the soul takes flight,
Through whispered winds in the silent night.
An interlude where thoughts unwind,
In the gentle embrace of peace we find.

Moments of clarity, brief but bright,
Fleeting glimpses of pure delight.
The heartbeats echo, a rhythmic song,
In the symphony where we all belong.

Time pauses with a soft refrain,
Washing away the dust of pain.
In the quiet spaces, we dare to dream,
Flowing like water in a silver stream.

Connection blooms in the heart's deep care,
Fragments of life suspended in air.
Here in this harmony, we feel whole,
An eternal dance, the interlude of the soul.

So let us savor these breaths, divine,
In the tapestry of life, we intertwine.
For in these moments, we truly live,
In the interlude of the soul, we forgive.

Enigma of the Lost

In twilight realms where secrets hide,
Whispers of the lost walk side by side.
Shattered pieces of a silent past,
Resonate softly, their echoes vast.

Footprints fading on ancient stones,
Stories untold in forgotten tones.
A labyrinth of dreams, tangled and wild,
Where the heart of the wanderer is just a child.

Mysteries weave through the fabric of time,
Searching for meaning in silent rhyme.
The enigma unfolds with each careful step,
In shadows of memory, we softly wept.

Yet traces linger, though paths obscure,
Yearning for moments that feel so pure.
So we seek the light in each lost embrace,
In the enigma of the lost, we find our place.

With every sigh, the past reclaims,
The flickering sparks of forgotten names.
In this journey of finding what's past,
We learn that the lost are never truly cast.

Cadence of Connexion

In whispers soft, the moments blend,
Notes of laughter, a symphony's end.
Echoes linger, a dance in the light,
Hearts entwined, through day and night.

A tapestry woven, threads of the past,
Links of our journeys, forever to last.
Every glance shared, a story to tell,
In the silence, we know all is well.

Rhythms of life, in sync we find,
A harmony crafted, two souls aligned.
In fleeting shadows, a bond takes flight,
Together we soar, through errors and right.

Time flows gently, a river so wide,
With every bend, we travel side by side.
A chorus of dreams, as colors collide,
In the cadence of connection, we abide.

Whims of Time's Hand

Time dances lightly, a fleeting embrace,
Moments like ripples, we chase in their grace.
Each second a whisper, a soft, gentle sway,
In the whims of its hand, we find our way.

Seasons unspooled, like threads from a loom,
Each tick of the clock, we weave into bloom.
A tapestry vibrant, in hues of our dreams,
Lost in the current, or so it seems.

Yesterday's echoes, today's fond refrain,
The laughter of children, the love and the pain.
Memories linger, like stars in the night,
In the whims of time, we seek our light.

Moments uncharted, horizons so wide,
We gather our hopes, and let them decide.
With each fleeting heartbeat, our stories expand,
In this dance of existence, we take a stand.

The Pulse of What Was

In quiet reflection, the past gently sighs,
A pulse ever-present, beneath twilight skies.
Whispers of yesterdays linger in air,
In the cadence of memory, we find the rare.

Fragments of laughter, like shards of the sun,
Each flicker a journey, where we have run.
The heartbeat of history, wise and profound,
In the pulse of what was, kinship is found.

Through shadows of ages, we wander and roam,
Finding our place in the fabric of home.
With every lost moment, we cherish the gain,
In the pulse of the past, we dance through the rain.

Time weaves its story, a thread to the now,
In the echoes of ages, we take a bow.
With roots planted deep, and branches that sway,
In the pulse of our being, we're never far away.

Breaths Beneath the Surface

Beneath the water's calm, a world concealed,
In whispers of currents, the heart is revealed.
Each breath a journey, a silent embrace,
In depths of the ocean, we find our place.

The glimmer of scales, in shadows they play,
Dancing with tides, in twilight's soft sway.
Waves of reflection, a mirror unfolds,
In the breath of the water, our story is told.

Every ripple, a heartbeat, a song of the sea,
In the depths of our souls, where we long to be.
Cradled by whispers, we float and we dive,
In the breaths of the surface, we come alive.

Emerging from depths, like stars in the night,
Each breath we take, ignites our sight.
With echoes of water, we find our tune,
In the dance of existence, beneath the moon.

Whispers of Forgotten Days

In the quiet corners, secrets lie,
Lost in echoes of a soft goodbye.
Memories linger like a gentle breeze,
Fleeting moments that time can't seize.

Beneath the stars where dreams once danced,
The heart remembers, though fate had chanced.
Fragments of laughter, shadows of tears,
Carried softly through the fleeting years.

Old photographs with faded smiles,
Tell of journeys across endless miles.
Each whispered story, a lover's plea,
Binding the past to what used to be.

The silence speaks in hushed tones,
Revealing paths that we have known.
A tapestry woven from threads of time,
In every stitch, an unsung rhyme.

So let the whispers of life remain,
Cradled softly in joy and pain.
For in forgotten days, we find our way,
Guided gently by light's soft sway.

Reverberations of the Past

In the stillness, echoes return,
Ghosts of laughter, heartaches that burn.
Footsteps linger on cobblestone,
Tales of a heart that once felt home.

Time's gentle touch leaves a trace,
A reminder of love's tender grace.
Whispers swirl within the air,
Each note a song of love laid bare.

Beneath the surface of our dreams,
Lie the shadows of ancient themes.
A symphony played on distant shores,
Humming softly, forever endures.

As the moonlight spills on forgotten lanes,
It carries with it the joy and pains.
The heart deciphers the song of days,
Finding solace in the silent ways.

Through the ages, the past informs,
Shaping our lives like raging storms.
In the reverberation, we lose and find,
Threads of time intertwined.

Shadows of Time's Embrace

In twilight's hush, the shadows grow,
Whispered secrets that we must know.
Time cradles all within its arms,
Guarding histories, with tender charms.

Old trees murmur where ancients tread,
Stories woven in silken thread.
Every leaf a memory of grace,
In the stillness of time's embrace.

Moments captured in a fleeting sigh,
Love not forgotten, it doesn't die.
Against the canvas of the night,
Shadows dance in the soft moonlight.

A tapestry of light and dark,
Every heartbeat leaves a mark.
In the silence, we find our place,
Entwined forever in time's embrace.

So let time's shadow softly guide,
Leading us where our dreams reside.
For in its arms, we learn to see,
The beauty that is yet to be.

Murmurs Beneath the Surface

In the depths, a gentle stir,
Whispers of a world that once were.
Beneath the waves, secrets sleep,
Guarded treasures, silent and deep.

The currents speak in ancient tongues,
Tales of lives, both old and young.
Each ripple carries hidden lore,
Murmurs echoing from the ocean's floor.

Beneath the calm lies a stormy past,
Winds of change that forever last.
In the shadows, the truth reveals,
Layers of time, ancient appeals.

As we dive into the darkened blue,
Murmurs rise, an enticing view.
The heart listens, the soul finds peace,
In depths where all forgotten cease.

So let the whispers of the deep,
Awaken dreams that softly seep.
For beneath the surface, all aligns,
Time's embrace within our vines.

Threads of Light and Shadow

In the dance of dusk and dawn,
Whispers weave a silent song.
Shadows stretch, then softly yawn,
While light reveals where dreams belong.

Glimmers spark within the night,
Guiding paths we can't ignore.
Each breath twines the dark and light,
A tapestry we all explore.

Fleeting moments in between,
Threads entwined, a story spun.
In the chaos, pure and clean,
We find solace, two as one.

Bound by dreams, we thread and weave,
Through the fabric of our fate.
In the light, we learn to grieve,
In the shadow, we create.

Every heartbeat, every sigh,
Marks the passage of our time.
Through the laughter, through the cry,
We embrace the intertime.

The Nostalgic Lament

In the attic, dust settles slow,
Whispers drift on golden air.
Echoes of a time we know,
Memories beyond compare.

Sunlight dances on the floor,
Every beam a fleeting smile.
In my heart, it lingers more,
Haunting me for just a while.

Childhood laughter, friends we knew,
Seasons wrapped in autumn's grace.
Each soft glance, a dream come true,
Captured in a warm embrace.

Now the silence fills the room,
Shadows claim the space we shared.
Yearning for the past to bloom,
In the echoes, I have bared.

Yet in sorrow, beauty gleams,
Woven through the tears I've shed.
Every loss, a thread of dreams,
In the heart, they're never dead.

Flickers of Truth

In the corners of the mind,
Fleeting thoughts like fireflies.
Searching for what's hard to find,
Truths that shimmer, then disguise.

Moments lost in shattered glass,
Reflecting all we try to chase.
Every wound, a mark to pass,
Flickers show a different face.

Words unspoken twist the air,
Caught in webs of what we fear.
But beneath the weight of care,
Lies the truth we hold so dear.

In the quiet, answers breathe,
Carved in time, a subtle song.
Lessons learned, we dare to leave,
Guiding us where we belong.

Though the night may stretch so long,
Stars will guide our broken way.
In the dark, we find our song,
Flickers of the dawn's bright ray.

Requiem for a Dream

In the silence of the night,
Dreams once bright begin to fade.
Fleeting visions, lost from sight,
In the shadows, choices made.

Whispers linger in the dark,
Echoes of a life once whole.
Every heartbeat leaves a mark,
Tracing paths that take their toll.

Hope was born from fragile light,
But the dawn can feel so far.
Every wish, a fading flight,
Once I reached for every star.

Yet in loss, there's something gained,
Lessons carved from joy and pain.
Every tear, a truth unchained,
In the heart, they still remain.

So I gather what is left,
Crafting beauty from the ache.
In the silence, find the deft,
Requiem for what's at stake.

Chronicles of the Invisible

In whispers of the night so deep,
Secrets of shadows softly creep.
The unseen tales of days gone by,
Awakening echoes, a silent sigh.

Veils of mist in the moon's soft glow,
Memories linger, they ebb and flow.
Through forgotten paths where phantoms tread,
Stories untold in silence spread.

In corners where the lost souls dwell,
Each fleeting moment, a magic spell.
Chronicles written in the stars above,
Ink of dreams and whispers of love.

A dance of shadows beneath the trees,
Carried away on a gentle breeze.
Invisible ties that bind the past,
Holding us close; shadows are cast.

In the hush of dusk where they reside,
Timeless guardians, they gently guide.
Through the tapestry of night and day,
Chronicles woven in shades of gray.

Shades of Forgotten Glory

In ruins of time where the echoes play,
Shades of glory have faded away.
Once shining bright like the morning sun,
Now memories linger, their race long run.

Golden halls where laughter rang clear,
Now silence whispers, a distant cheer.
Fragments of stories left untold,
In shadows of ages, the past unfolds.

Heroes of yore, with courage displayed,
Have slipped into dreams where shadows wade.
Their deeds entwined in the fabric of night,
A tapestry woven with lost, fading light.

Time flows like rivers, relentless and cold,
Carrying stories of ages bold.
In the heart of dusk, their spirits rise,
Dancing in twilight under starry skies.

Remember the echoes, the lives that were lived,
In shades of forgotten, the lessons they give.
Though glory may fade, their legacies stay,
In whispers of time, they're never far away.

The Solitary Resonance

In a quiet room, silence speaks loud,
A solitary soul stands tall, unbowed.
Echoes of thoughts flutter and fly,
Deep in the heart, where dreams sigh.

Waves of solitude gently crash,
Moments of stillness, like lightning flash.
Each whisper resounds with clarity profound,
A melody sweet, in silence is found.

Time stretches thin like a shimmering thread,
Woven from hopes, where the lost fears tread.
In the pulse of the night, a heartbeat plays,
The sound of a soul in its quiet maze.

Lonely notes on a stringed old guitar,
Each strum a story, near and far.
In the embrace of night's gentle hand,
Resonance dances across the land.

Though solitude reigns in the moon's soft glow,
Seeds of connection begin to grow.
In silence, we find what we all seek,
A symphony waiting, in whispers, we speak.

Time's Silent Chorus

In the depths of the night, soft whispers rise,
Time sings gently, beneath starlit skies.
Each tick of the clock holds stories untold,
A silent chorus of moments bold.

Songs of the past linger in the air,
Melodies drifting as we drift and stare.
In the dance of the leaves, the rustling trees,
Time's gentle rhythm carries on the breeze.

Hours like lovers slip through our hands,
Chasing the sun across shifting sands.
In twilight's embrace, they pause and blend,
A soft caress as they come to an end.

Echoes of laughter, the sighs of the lost,
Every note weighs with the love and the cost.
In the heart of each moment, life comes alive,
As time's silent chorus begins to thrive.

The future awaits with a tender embrace,
While the past lingers here, an intricate lace.
In the silence of now, we hear their refrain,
Time's gentle chorus a sweet, subtle gain.

Along the River of Time

Gentle waters flow by,
Carrying whispers of days,
To the shore of dreams gone,
In twilight's warm haze.

Reflections of laughter,
Dance upon the crest,
As memories drift softly,
Finding their long-rest.

Each ripple a moment,
Flashing bright and clear,
Recalling the faces,
We hold so dear.

Seasons shift and sway,
In the current's embrace,
Time bends and twists,
In this sacred space.

And as the sun sets,
On this endless ride,
We gather the fragments,
That we carry with pride.

Arial Portraits of Memory

In hues of faded ink,
Reside our unseen tales,
Brush strokes of the past,
Drawn like whispered gales.

Through clouds of nostalgia,
We sketch the lives we led,
On pages full of dreams,
And paths we nearly tread.

Each portrait holds a story,
Framed under a sigh,
In the gallery of time,
Where echoes never die.

Colors blend and smudge,
In the heart's quiet space,
Charting the skies above,
That we dare to trace.

With each brush of memory,
We paint what once was true,
An artful reminder,
Of the me and you.

The Forgotten Arcana

In shadows of silence,
Lies wisdom long concealed,
Secrets weave through ages,
In patterns unrevealed.

Once sacred incantations,
Whispered by the wise,
Echo in the darkness,
Under twisting skies.

The lore of ancient times,
Resonates in dreams,
In forgotten tomes,
Where the magic gleams.

Each page a distant memory,
Of spells that changed the night,
Guarded by the echoes,
Of an elusive light.

We delve into the mysteries,
With hearts both brave and bold,
Unlocking the arcana,
Of treasures long untold.

Timeless Reverie

In the hush of twilight's glow,
Memories dance in soft shadows,
Whispers of dreams yet to unfold,
A tapestry of stories told.

Stars awaken in silent skies,
Glimmers of hope in each surprise,
Every moment a fleeting sigh,
Time drifts gently, passing by.

Echoes linger in the deep night,
A heartbeat lost in soft twilight,
Chasing reflections of the past,
In this realm, the die is cast.

Morning breaks with golden rays,
Painting memories of the days,
In this reverie, I will stay,
As time weaves dreams, come what may.

Restless spirits, eternal flight,
In the folds of endless night,
A timeless dance, we weave and spin,
In reverie, we are all akin.

Collage of Sighs

Fragments of life, scattered wide,
A collage formed from each tide,
Colors bleed, emotions sway,
In this gallery of the gray.

Silent whispers, echoes bold,
Stories hidden, love untold,
Each sigh captured, softly penned,
A bittersweet tale without end.

Mirrors shattered, dreams unmade,
In the light, the shadows fade,
Every breath a piece to find,
In this art, we are entwined.

Canvas draped with hues of night,
Chasing shadows, searching light,
Emotions bleed, they intertwine,
A collage framed in the divine.

Where hearts converge and silence sighs,
In this tapestry of our tries,
Each moment captured, bright or dim,
A life's collage, both frail and grim.

Glimpses of the Infinite

In the vastness, whispers call,
Glimpses of moments, big and small,
Each breath a thread of timeless grace,
Infinity held in a single space.

Stars align in cosmic dance,
Eternal rhythms, fate and chance,
In every heartbeat, echoes blend,
Glimpses where beginnings end.

Softly painted with fleeting hues,
Dreams uncountable, paths to choose,
The universe sings in quiet tone,
A symphony of the unknown.

Waves of light and fragments pure,
Crafting stories that endure,
In the infinite, we find our way,
Guided by night, leading to day.

What is time but a gentle tide,
Carrying us on a graceful ride?
In glimpses, we seek what lies within,
The infinite dance, where we begin.

Shattered Reflections

Mirrors cracked, visions askew,
Shattered dreams slip from view,
In the glass, we see the shards,
Fragments of truth, hiding hard.

Each piece a memory, sharp and bright,
A story lost in fading light,
When laughter echoes, hearts collide,
In shattered reflections, we confide.

Torn between what was and is,
A puzzle of self, an endless quiz,
In this chaos, we find our grace,
Embracing the cracks, the lost embrace.

Through broken glass, we seek the whole,
A million pieces, one shared soul,
In reflections scattered, we explore,
Shattered yet shining, forever more.

With every fracture, a lesson learned,
In each heartbreak, passion burned,
Through shattered reflections, we find our way,
In the mosaic of night and day.

Echoing in the Abyss

In shadows deep, whispers call,
A haunting song, a silent pall.
The depths reply with sighs of old,
Echoes lost in darkness cold.

Faint glimmers flash, then fade from sight,
Phantoms dance in fading light.
Heartbeats thrum, the void reflects,
Memory's grip, the soul connects.

A journey found beneath the tide,
Where secrets in stillness hide.
With every breath, the abyss speaks,
A truth that's found in silence bleak.

Whispers merge, a symphony,
In the heart of mystery.
Lost in echoes, yearning
For a truth that's yet returning.

Through the dark, the spirit roams,
In twilight paths, it seeks its home.
In each echo, stories lie,
Awaiting those who dare to fly.

When Time Stood Still

A moment captured, frozen tight,
In the hush before the night.
Seconds linger, hearts entwine,
In this dance, our souls align.

Beneath the stars, whispers flow,
Where every breath begins to grow.
A stillness found in fleeting grace,
Time bows down, a soft embrace.

Eyes meet on the edge of fate,
In this pause, we contemplate.
Every heartbeat echoes here,
In the silence, love draws near.

Through the ages, moments blend,
In every start, we find an end.
Yet in this space, forever stays,
A cherished glance, a timeless gaze.

When all is quiet, life reveals,
The magic that stillness heals.
In whispered dreams, we shall remain,
In the pause where love can reign.

Harmonies of the Forgotten

Silent echoes of days gone by,
Songs of old that fill the sky.
Melodies that drift like clouds,
In lost dreams, their voice enshrouds.

Through the mist of yesterday,
Harmonies of light decay.
Faded notes on windswept shores,
Call to hearts that long for more.

In every chord, a tale unfolds,
Whispers rich with love retold.
The forgotten still have claim,
In our hearts, they spark the flame.

As twilight falls, they softly sing,
In the silence, their echoes cling.
Each note a memory alive,
In forgotten songs, we thrive.

With gentle chords that stir the soul,
Planting seeds where shadows roll.
In remembrance, we find our way,
Harmonies that forever sway.

Fluidity of Being

In the river of thought, we flow,
Beneath the surface, currents grow.
Each wave a shift in the mind's sea,
A dance of thoughts, of you and me.

Life's fleeting moments like sand,
Shift and shimmer, elusive hand.
We grasp at time as it slips away,
In the fluid embrace of day.

Every breath a fleeting sigh,
In the breeze, our spirits fly.
Lost in the ebb, we find our ground,
In flowing waters, truth unbound.

Each challenge shapes the stream of fate,
Molding pathways that resonate.
We bend and sway, the journey's art,
In fluidity lies the heart.

From one moment to the next,
Life's gentle curve, we must respect.
Embrace the change, let the river steer,
In its flow, find love sincere.

Songs of the Long Forgotten

Whispers dance in the twilight air,
Faint echoes of lives once lived,
Stars blink, as if to share,
Memories that time has sieved.

Shadows weave through ancient trees,
Soft murmurs of pain and glee,
Carry tales on the evening breeze,
Of a world we cease to see.

A melody lost in the dark,
Haunting notes linger still,
Each heartbeat leaves a mark,
On the silence of the hill.

Lullabies of forgotten days,
Comments on the life once known,
Roots gripping in tangled ways,
Yet seeds of hope have grown.

With every chord we breathe new life,
Turning ashes into flame,
To erase the lingering strife,
And remember each name.

The Pulse of Silent Stories

In shadows deep where secrets lie,
Pulses thrum in the still of night,
Each heartbeat whispers a sigh,
Revealing dreams that take flight.

Ancient stones hum with past grace,
Murals hidden beneath the skin,
Every crack tells of a place,
Where forgotten heartbeats begin.

Tales linger in the quiet air,
Flickering like a candle's glow,
With every breath, a silent prayer,
For the stories only they know.

Hands reach out through time's embrace,
Tracing fingers on history's sheet,
To uncover forgotten face,
And share love's tender beat.

In the void, pulses ignite,
Sparking dreams that refuse to fade,
Lost in the depths of night,
Resurrecting memories made.

Fragments in the Breeze

Caught in the currents, pieces drift,
Shards of moments long ago,
Each fragment holds a timeless gift,
In the soft whispers of the flow.

Wings of paper, stories in flight,
Carried by winds of chance and change,
Reflecting shadows in fading light,
Reshaping life in a dance so strange.

With every rustle, dreams collide,
Painting truths on empty skies,
Memories surge like an incoming tide,
Under the watchful, silent eyes.

Gathering tales from laughter's grace,
And sorrows woven through the night,
Fragments hidden in every place,
Yearning for warmth, for light.

In the breeze, an echo calls,
A soft reminder of what has been,
Each whisper holds as silence falls,
A promise of what lies unseen.

Tides of Unwritten History

Waves roll gently on sandy shores,
Carrying legends yet untold,
Each crest a whisper, pure as pours,
Of worlds that time cannot hold.

Beneath the surface, stories sleep,
Waiting for the call of the moon,
A tide that breaks, fierce and deep,
To stir the night in timeless bloom.

Seashells cradle voices lost,
Echoes gliding on the swell,
Each grain of sand computes the cost,
Of forgotten dreams that fell.

A canvas formed by fleeting waves,
Sketching characters of fate,
Weaving legends, what history saves,
In the lull of the ocean's gate.

With every tide, a tale reborn,
Whispered by winds, fierce and free,
Tracing paths of the forlorn,
In the deep, a mystery.

Resonance of Lost Journeys

Footsteps fade on the winding road,
Whispers of dreams in the twilight mode.
Paths once bright, now dimmed by time,
Memories linger like silent rhyme.

The sun dips low, shadows stretch long,
A heart still beats to a world once strong.
Tread softly where the echoes dwell,
Each step a tale, each sigh a shell.

Clouds roll in with silver and gray,
Guide our thoughts as they drift away.
In the silence, the past unfolds,
Unraveling truths that fate once told.

Journeys lost, yet found in dreams,
Rivers whisper, as daylight beams.
The horizons call, beckoning wide,
To embrace the winds, let the heart decide.

In every turn, every missed call,
We trace the paths where shadows fall.
A map of hope, sketched in sand,
Each grain a story, each footfall planned.

Reflections in the Stillness

In quiet pools, the world reflects,
Thoughts drift softly, as silence connects.
Gentle ripples break the calm,
Nature's breath, a soothing balm.

Time slows down, embracing the night,
Stars shimmer softly, a guiding light.
In her arms, the weary find peace,
Whispers of dreams that never cease.

The moonlight dances on silver streams,
Revealing truths behind the seams.
In the stillness, we find our way,
Carried by night till the dawn of day.

Every heartbeat, a rhythmic song,
In stillness deep, where we belong.
Nature speaks in hushed tones,
With every sigh, the heart intones.

Reflections linger, time stands still,
In moments quiet, we breathe at will.
Lost in thought, we gently sway,
Finding solace in the gray.

The Sound of Remembered Dreams

Faint whispers weave through the night,
Carrying tales in the soft moonlight.
Dreams once vivid, now shadows cast,
Echoes of moments forever past.

Through the silence, the mind recalls,
Laughter and tears within the walls.
Fluttering wings of hope in flight,
Kisses of dawn, kissing goodnight.

The sound of laughter, a distant chime,
Holding the softness of lost time.
In every heartbeat, a story sings,
Memories held in fragile wings.

With every sigh, the past returns,
Fire of longing, the spirit burns.
In shadows deep, our voices combine,
Crafting a symphony, celestial line.

Waves of emotion, the heart does greet,
In the still of night, bitter and sweet.
The sound of dreams, they softly call,
A timeless echo that binds us all.

Vibrations of Forgotten Voices

In the silence, a faint sound stirs,
Whispers of faces, time now blurs.
Laughter lingers, a distant tune,
Memories dance beneath the moon.

Faint vibrations hum in the air,
Forgotten voices, light as a prayer.
Echoes of love in shadows play,
Stories woven in night and day.

Each word spoken, a pulse of heart,
In every silence, we find our part.
Winds carry tales from far-off shores,
Of lives once lived, now open doors.

Time rolls on, yet we still hear,
Voices of those we hold so dear.
In gentle whispers, they remain,
Vibrations lasting, never in vain.

Through quiet moments, we pause to feel,
The weight of history, tender and real.
In echoes soft, our spirits rise,
Vibrations of love beneath endless skies.

A Tapestry of Time

Threads of gold weave through the night,
Whispers of stories tucked away tight.
Moments dance in the quiet air,
Echoes of laughter, beyond compare.

Seasons turn with a gentle grace,
Each one leaving its soft embrace.
Memories linger, a sweet refrain,
Bound by the joy and tempered pain.

In the loom of dreams, we find our way,
Through the shadowed paths of yesterday.
Each stitch a heartbeat, strong and clear,
A tapestry rich, as we draw near.

Time wraps us in its endless loop,
Carrying hopes in a silent scoop.
From dawn to dusk, we weave our fate,
With every breath, we celebrate.

So here we stand, together entwined,
In the tapestry, our souls aligned.
With threads of love, we craft the night,
Eternal weaver, dreams take flight.

Fragmented Harmonies

Notes are scattered like fallen leaves,
Melodies lost in the softest eves.
Each sound a whisper, a tale to tell,
In the space between, we find our spell.

Moments collide, rhythms collide,
Fragments of beauty we can't abide.
In silence, echoes begin to bloom,
As shadows sway, dispelling gloom.

Chords that linger in twilight's breath,
Woven together, transcending death.
Though shattered pieces may seek to stray,
Harmony rises, leading the way.

Fingers dance on the strings of fate,
Creating music we cultivate.
In every sorrow, in every song,
We stitch our hearts, where we belong.

Through the chaos, we find our rhyme,
Fragmented lives in the hands of time.
Let the notes fly, let the heart sway,
In this symphony, forever stay.

Resonating Solitude

In the quietude where shadows play,
Whispers of dreams softly drift away.
Walls of silence cradle the mind,
In solitude's grasp, treasures we find.

Stars sing to the silent expanse,
Inviting the heart to a gentle dance.
Embers of thoughts flicker and glow,
Lighting the corners where shadows flow.

Time sits still in this sacred space,
Echoes of longing gently embrace.
In the solitude, we learn to feel,
The depth of silence, the heart's conceal.

With every breath, a story unwinds,
In the stillness, the soul aligns.
The weight of the world begins to lift,
In resonating solitude, we gift.

So here we revel, alone yet whole,
In the quiet symphony, we find our role.
For in this moment, so soft and sweet,
Solitude whispers, and time is complete.

Embrace of Time's Whirl

Time spins a tale in a dizzying dance,
Moments entwined, lost in a trance.
Days fade softly into the night,
In the whirl of time, we find our light.

Seasons breeze like a lover's sigh,
Dancing through clouds in the vast sky.
Echoing laughter, tears that fall,
In time's embrace, we answer the call.

Each tick a heartbeat, a precious gift,
Guiding our souls through the gentle rift.
Holding on tightly as moments fade,
In the embrace of time, memories are made.

Fleeting seconds weave past and present,
Creating a tapestry, rich and pleasant.
Through every turn, we find our way,
In the labyrinth of time, we choose to stay.

So let us twirl in this sacred flow,
In love's soft cradle, we gently glow.
For in the embrace of time's sweet whirl,
Life's precious moments unfurl.

Cadence of Fleeting Moments

In shadows cast by the fading light,
We dance beneath the stars so bright.
Each heartbeat whispers tales untold,
A tapestry of dreams unfolds.

Time spins softly, a lullaby,
Moments drift, like clouds on high.
We gather memories, thread by thread,
In the silence where words have fled.

Echoes linger, the past entwined,
Every heartbeat a reminder kind.
We chase the fleeting, hold it tight,
In the gentle embrace of night.

With every sigh, we learn to grow,
In precious seconds, love will flow.
A cadence soft, a swift refrain,
In fleeting moments, joy and pain.

As roses bloom, then fade away,
We grasp the now, and then, one day,
The dance of life, a fleeting chance,
In the beauty of this timeless dance.

The Symphony of What Was

Notes of laughter, echoes of tears,
A symphony played across the years.
In every chord, a memory lies,
A sonnet sung beneath the skies.

Time composes with graceful hands,
Melodies linger where silence stands.
The past resounds, a haunting tune,
Under the watchful gaze of the moon.

Harmony weaves through love's embrace,
A thousand stories, each a trace.
The wind carries whispers, soft and sweet,
As echoes of yesterday softly meet.

In the silence, a melody grows,
The heart remembers what time bestows.
Each note a brushstroke, vibrant and wide,
In the symphony, we cannot hide.

As seasons change and turn to dust,
We hold the notes in gentle trust.
The music of life, rich and deep,
In the symphony of what we keep.

Melodies of Memories Lost

Pages turn in a weathered book,
Tales of love in every nook.
The melody drifts like a sigh,
In the spaces where dreams lie.

Faded photographs, whispers of time,
In every shadow, a fleeting rhyme.
We search for echoes, lost in sight,
In the dusk of fading light.

Sweet melodies of laughter ring,
Yet deep inside, a sorrow clings.
We gather fragments, piece by piece,
A symphony that yearns for peace.

In every heartbeat, a story waits,
Time unravels, it hesitates.
As memories fade, we hold them close,
In the quiet, where longing grows.

With every note, a tear may fall,
Yet in the silence, we hear the call.
The melodies linger, soft and lost,
In echoes of love, we pay the cost.

Chronicles in the Wind

Whispers carried on the breeze,
Tales of old among the trees.
Chronicles penned in nature's tome,
Every rustle speaks of home.

Through valleys deep and mountains high,
Stories linger, never die.
In each breath of the twilight air,
We find the words, silent but fair.

Time unravels like endless thread,
Paths we've taken, journeys led.
In the quiet, we listen in,
To the tales the winds have spun.

As stars glimmer in the night sky,
Chronicles of life drift and fly.
Every sigh a story told,
In the ink of time, bright and bold.

The winds will carry us along,
With every gust, we sing our song.
In these chronicles, bold and vast,
We find our future within the past.

Chasing Faint Illusions

In the morning mist we roam,
Seeking shadows, far from home.
Echoes of dreams that softly fade,
Chasing whispers in the glade.

Fleeting visions dance around,
Lost in silence, barely found.
Threads of hope, so thin and frail,
Guiding hearts on a winding trail.

Through the twilight, shadows creep,
Secret promises we keep.
Illusions flicker, then they flee,
Yet our hearts beat endlessly.

Endless paths in twilight's glow,
Lost in places none may know.
Chasing echoes, through and through,
Faint illusions, always new.

But in the night, as dreams reside,
We'll hold the light, let hope abide.
Through faint illusions, we will chase,
Finding solace in the space.

Starlit Whispers

Underneath the velvet skies,
Moonlit secrets softly rise.
Whispers cradled in the night,
Stars confiding, pure delight.

Through the branches, shadows sway,
Nature's lullaby at play.
Every twinkle, every gleam,
Holds a promise, holds a dream.

In the stillness, hearts unite,
Starlit paths, our guiding light.
Voices murmur in the dark,
Each a wish, each a spark.

As constellations trace their lines,
Ancient stories, love resigns.
Softly echoing the past,
In the night, forever cast.

So let us wander, hand in hand,
Through the whispers of this land.
In the starlight, we will find,
Peace and magic intertwined.

Resonating Futures

In the canvas of our dreams,
Future's light softly gleams.
Each decision, a brushstroke fair,
Painting visions in the air.

Voices echo, choices call,
Building bridges, weaving all.
New horizons lie ahead,
Paths we tread, where hope is fed.

In the symphony of time,
We discover, hearts will chime.
Every moment, rich and bright,
Resonating through the night.

Together we will pave the way,
Chasing shadows, come what may.
Future's tapestry unfolds,
In stories that have yet been told.

So let us leap beyond the line,
Into futures, bright, divine.
With every heartbeat, we will rise,
Resonating through the skies.

Memories in Echo

In the corners of our mind,
Fleeting whispers left behind.
Memories dance like autumn leaves,
Stories held in every breeze.

Time concludes, yet still they play,
Fragments scattered, day by day.
Face of laughter, taste of tears,
Carried softly, through the years.

Echoes linger, sharp and clear,
Telling tales we hold so dear.
In the silence, heartbeats swell,
Memories weave their secret spell.

Through the corridors of time,
Every step, a whispered rhyme.
Past and present intertwined,
In the echoes, light we find.

So let us treasure, hold them tight,
In the shadows, find the light.
Memories sparkle, hearts will glow,
In the echoes, love will grow.

Reverberations of the Heart

In shadows deep where secrets dwell,
The heart beats soft, a hidden spell.
Whispers of love in twilight's glow,
Echo through time, where feelings flow.

A gentle pulse, a sacred dance,
In every glance, a fleeting chance.
Memories linger, caught in the air,
Reverberations of what we share.

Silent promises held so tight,
A flickering flame in the still of night.
Between the beats, a longing sigh,
For every wish that passed us by.

The rhythm swells, a soothing balm,
In chaotic worlds, it finds its calm.
Notes of the heart, soft and pure,
In every heartbeat, we endure.

As time unfolds, the echoes play,
Guiding us through the night and day.
In every whisper, we find our part,
The beautiful song of the heart.

A Symphony of Shadows

Beneath the moon's soft silvery light,
Shadows dance, taking flight.
With silent grace, they intertwine,
A symphony where spirits align.

Flickering flames cast stories old,
In twilight hues of amber and gold.
Each shadow tells a tale anew,
Of dreams once bright that faded from view.

They waltz across the walls of night,
An elegant show, a haunting sight.
With every move, they softly sigh,
A lullaby to the stars on high.

In stillness shared, we find our peace,
Where shadows weave and sorrows cease.
A tapestry spun of light and dark,
In this quiet realm, we leave our mark.

As dawn breaks through the veil of dreams,
Shadows retreat, or so it seems.
Yet in our hearts, they still reside,
A symphony where love won't hide.

Trails of Yesterday

On winding paths where footsteps fade,
Echoes linger, memories made.
Each gentle breeze whispers low,
Of places gone, where we used to go.

Sunset hues paint the sky anew,
Reminders of what we once knew.
With every turn, a story unfolds,
Of laughter shared and courage bold.

Leaves fall gently, a soft goodbye,
To seasons past that never die.
In every rustle, a whisper calls,
Recalling love that never falls.

Time may fade the vibrant scene,
But hearts will hold where we have been.
Through trails of yesterday, we roam,
Finding fragments of our home.

In twilight's glow, we search for light,
Embracing shadows, we face the night.
For in each step, a thread we weave,
A tapestry of all we believe.

The Sound of Silence

In stillness lies a sacred sound,
Where peace and whispers can be found.
A canvas blank, a tranquil sea,
The sound of silence, wild and free.

Beneath the stars, the world retreats,
In quietude, my spirit meets.
With every breath, the silence speaks,
In soft embraces, my soul seeks.

Through gentle winds, I hear the call,
Of nature's pulse, the heartbeat's thrall.
A melody spun from moonlit sky,
Where echoes of love never die.

The hush of dawn, the twilight's dream,
In shadows deep, we find our theme.
A symphony held in every sigh,
In the sound of silence, we learn to fly.

So let us linger, breath and pause,
In silent moments, find our cause.
For in this stillness, hearts ignite,
The sound of silence guides our flight.

The Afterglow of Being

In the quiet night, stars align,
Soft whispers linger, secrets entwine.
Moments of peace, where shadows play,
The afterglow lingers, fading day.

Fragments of dreams dance in the air,
Embers of laughter, beyond compare.
Life's gentle hum, a soothing song,
In the afterglow, we all belong.

Beneath the moon, hearts softly glow,
Threads of our stories start to flow.
Each heartbeat echoes, tender and true,
In the afterglow, it's me and you.

Colors fade but memories stay,
In twilight's embrace, we find our way.
With every breath, love's warmth we find,
In the afterglow, souls intertwined.

As dawn approaches, light breaks free,
The afterglow whispers, "Come dance with me."
With open hearts, let the journey begin,
In the glow of life, together we win.

Unraveled Tapestries

Threads of life blend, colors collide,
Stories told where truths cannot hide.
Woven with care, yet fraying at seams,
Unraveled tapestries, lost in dreams.

Fingers trace paths where fibers were spun,
Every knot holds the weight of the sun.
Patterns emerge from a tangled mess,
Unraveled stories, both pain and bliss.

The loom of time, it sways and bends,
We mend the fabric, yet it contends.
Each tug reveals, each pull sets free,
Unraveled tapestries, meant to be.

Fragments of laughter, patches of tears,
Binding our spirits through all the years.
In every stitch, a tale we find,
Unraveled tapestries, hearts combined.

As we unwind, new colors arise,
In the tapestry's heart, love never lies.
Embrace the weave, let the journey show,
An endless story, in threads that flow.

Simmering Emotions

Bubbles burst in every heart,
Feelings dance, a vibrant art.
Whispers of passion, soft and low,
Simmering emotions, wait and grow.

The heat of longing, a flicker of light,
In shadows they linger, ready to ignite.
From gentle murmurs to a storm's prose,
Simmering emotions, the heart's throes.

Layers unfold, each one a tale,
Crafting connections that never pale.
In silence, they brew, ready to show,
The essence of love, its ebb and flow.

Fleeting glances, a spark in the air,
Embers of hope, floating somewhere.
On this journey, we've much to know,
Simmering emotions, steady and slow.

Through every taste, we learn and grow,
In the pot of life, feelings bestow.
With hearts wide open, together we glow,
In simmering emotions, let love overflow.

Traces in Twilight

As daylight fades, shadows creep near,
Soft whispers echo, memories dear.
Traces of laughter, danced in the light,
Fleeting as stars in the velvet night.

The world turns golden, a sweet embrace,
Silhouettes linger, time cannot erase.
Footprints in sand wash away with the tide,
Traces in twilight, where dreams abide.

Glimmers of hope in the dusky air,
Each fading moment, love's tender flare.
In twilight's glow, our stories unite,
Traces of magic, hidden from sight.

As night unfolds, secrets are shared,
In the hush of dusk, we feel unprepared.
Yet in that stillness, our hearts find flight,
Traces in twilight, everything feels right.

Embrace the whispers, let spirits soar,
In the light of the moon, we dream once more.
Drawing from shadows, we take our flight,
In traces of twilight, love shines bright.

Murmurs of the Ancients

Whispers in the breeze,
Echoes of time gone by,
Stories etched in stone,
Lessons from those who fly.

Beneath the ancient trees,
Roots dig deep in the earth,
Their limbs stretch wide and free,
Guardians of wisdom's worth.

Misty hills hold their tales,
Cascading through the years,
Carried on waves of sound,
Provoking silent tears.

In shadows of the dusk,
Memories softly blend,
Brushing against our skin,
A message without end.

Their wisdom calls to us,
As the night starts to fall,
We listen with open hearts,
To the ancients' gentle call.

Footprints in the Sand

Waves wash on the shore,
Leaving traces of the past,
Each step, a fleeting mark,
Ephemeral, yet vast.

The sun begins to set,
Colors bleed into the sea,
Each footprint tells a story,
Of who we used to be.

Glistening with the tide,
Memories ebb and flow,
With every rise and fall,
Our journey's ebbing glow.

The wind whispers secrets,
Carrying dreams held tight,
Footprints fade with each wave,
But the heart remembers night.

As we walk this shoreline,
We embrace what slips away,
For every step we leave,
Shapes the dawn of a new day.

Polaroids of Past Lives

Snapshots in a drawer,
Faded faces tell of yore,
Each a glimpse, a whisper,
Of lives that came before.

Sunshine on the river,
Captured joy in still frames,
Frozen laughs, a heartbeat,
Life lived without the names.

Dusty corners hold dreams,
Moments thick with time's grace,
Fleeting glances, captured,
In a fast-paced, slow embrace.

Each frame a portal opens,
To worlds once bright and grand,
Where laughter echoes softly,
As we gently understand.

Though years may blur the images,
And colors fade to gray,
The feelings held within them,
Forever find their way.

Fragments of Memory

Scattered pieces linger,
Like leaves upon the ground,
Bits of laughter, whispers,
In the silence, they're found.

Chasing shadows of youth,
Through corridors of the mind,
Each turn reveals a story,
Of what we've left behind.

Mosaic of moments,
Fragile and intertwined,
Every glance, a treasure,
In the heart, they're enshrined.

Dusty books hold secrets,
Pages turn without a sound,
With every line recited,
Old find new ground.

We gather these fragments,
Constructing what we claim,
In the tapestry of life,
We seek to find our name.

Veils of the Unfathomable

In shadows deep the secrets dwell,
Behind the mist, a whispered spell.
Silken threads of time entwine,
In the dark, the stars align.

A journey starts where none can see,
With every breath, a mystery.
Veils of doubt, yet hope remains,
In the silence, truth still reigns.

An echo calls through endless night,
To chase the dreams that feel so right.
Embrace the shadows, let them guide,
Through veils of thoughts, let pain subside.

With every step, a path unfolds,
In the quiet, magic holds.
Dimensions bend and time allows,
To understand the sacred vows.

So linger here, where visions blend,
In darkness deep, we find the end.
For what is lost can still be found,
In veils of dreams, our souls unbound.

Faded Footsteps

Along the path where silence reigns,
Faded footprints tell of pains.
Ghostly trails in misty light,
Whispers linger through the night.

Each step a story, worn and old,
Of laughter shared and tales retold.
In every mark, a memory weeps,
The heart remembers, yet it keeps.

Through autumn leaves and winter's frost,
We calculate the love we lost.
Yet forward still the journey goes,
In faded steps, new life will grow.

The past is stitched into our seams,
Haunting us in all our dreams.
But in each tread, the future calls,
A dance of life that never stalls.

So trace the paths where shadows play,
In faded footsteps, find the way.
For every loss ignites a spark,
To guide us through the endless dark.

Dance of the Reverent Dust

In golden light, the dust does sway,
A quiet dance at close of day.
Particles of time take flight,
In reverence beneath the light.

They twirl and spin in cosmic grace,
Connecting worlds in soft embrace.
Each mote a dream, a story spun,
A fleeting glimpse of all that's done.

With gentle rhythm, they descend,
A whispering breeze, a timeless friend.
Through ancient halls and sacred ground,
In silence deep, the truths are found.

So let the dust in stillness flow,
A testament of what we know.
For in each dance of vibrant hue,
Lies a promise of life anew.

Embrace the swirl of twilight's bliss,
In the dance of dust, find solace.
For as they gather in the night,
They carry dreams into the light.

Layers of Yesterday's Echo

In layers thick, the echoes lie,
A tapestry of when and why.
Whispers linger in the air,
Of hopes and dreams that once were there.

The past unfolds in gentle waves,
Each story told, the heart still craves.
Memories wrapped in time's embrace,
Reflecting light on every face.

Through the shadows, visions dance,
Inviting thoughts, a fleeting chance.
To weave the present with the past,
To cherish moments that can last.

In layers deep, the silence roars,
Resounding through the open doors.
Each echo holds a truth to know,
A journey taken, a seed we sow.

So listen close to yesterday,
In echoes soft, find your own way.
For every layer, a heartbeat's sound,
In the depths of time, we're truly found.

Snippets from Yesteryears

Whispers of the past, a gentle sway,
Memories linger, they softly play.
Faded photographs, smiles in time,
Echoes of laughter, rhythm, and rhyme.

Familiar faces, warmth in their gaze,
Each story shared, like an endless maze.
Fragments of life that we hold so dear,
Snippets of yesterdays, crystal clear.

Time weaves its tale with delicate thread,
A tapestry rich with words left unsaid.
Each moment counts, in silence they bloom,
Treasured reminders, dispelling the gloom.

Gone are the days, yet here they remain,
In the heart's chamber, they still entertain.
Lost in the twilight, we find our way,
Guided by memories, come what may.

With every heartbeat, we live and we learn,
In the shadows of time, our passions burn.
Snippets of yesteryears, cherished and bright,
They dance in our minds, like stars in the night.

The Call of Distant Stars

In the quiet night, when the world sleeps,
The call of distant stars, a secret it keeps.
Twinkling lights, they beckon from afar,
Whispers of galaxies, dreams like a spar.

Endless cosmos, a tapestry wide,
Each pinprick of light, a heart open wide.
We chase after visions, on a celestial plane,
Finding our place in the vastness of rain.

Nebulas harbor, the colors collide,
Filling the void where our hopes abide.
Through telescopes gazing, we long to explore,
The secrets of time, and what lies in store.

Shooting stars race through the velvet sky,
Making wishes of hearts that dream and fly.
With every glimmer, there's a promise to hold,
Stories of stardust, forever retold.

Asleep in the night, the universe sighs,
Its vastness inspires, allows us to rise.
The call of distant stars, a hymn we compose,
In the fabric of space, our journey unfolds.

Layers of Existence

Life unfolds gently, like pages in time,
Layers of existence, a delicate rhyme.
Each heartbeat a story, each breath a profound,
The music of being, where wonders abound.

Moments like petals, unfold in the light,
Colors and textures blend day into night.
We search for our meaning, in whispers of air,
Unraveling layers, with tenderest care.

Connections we nurture, threads intertwined,
Binding us close, through the vast and the blind.
In silence we find, what words cannot say,
The essence of life, in shadows and play.

In chaos and order, we learn to reside,
Navigating paths that we often divide.
Layers of existence, reveal with each turn,
A mosaic of moments, for which we all yearn.

Through laughter and tears, we discover our way,
Embracing each layer, come what may.
In the garden of time, each flower will bloom,
In layers of existence, we find our room.

Soft Places in Time

There are soft places, tucked deep in our hearts,
Where memories settle, and time gently departs.
Cradled by shadows, warmth holds us near,
In those tender spaces, we conquer our fear.

Like dawn's gentle light, they softly appear,
Whispers of comfort, forever so near.
As moments pass by, they linger and sway,
Soft places in time, where we dare to stay.

The laughter of children, the stories they weave,
In the fabric of love, we learn to believe.
A touch, a smile, can unravel the storm,
In soft places of time, we are safe and warm.

With every heartbeat, we gather and grow,
Finding soft places, like rivers that flow.
Through joy and through sorrow, we learn to embrace,
The beauty of stillness, in time's tender grace.

So treasure those moments, both fleeting and rare,
For soft places in time are beyond compare.
They cradle our spirits, and guide our way home,
In tender reflections, together we roam.

The Unraveling Silence

In shadows deep, the quiet reigns,
A whispered breath, the stillness strains.
Each sound a ghost, it drifts away,
Holding the night, where echoes play.

Beneath the stars, a secret waits,
An unspoken truth that fate creates.
The silence weaves its careful thread,
In dreams where hearts have softly fled.

A canvas blank, yet filled with fears,
The lull of time will dry the tears.
In every pause, a story grows,
Within the silence, life bestows.

With open ears, we learn to hear,
The subtle calls that draw us near.
In silence lies the weight of choice,
A serenade, we find our voice.

Come walk this path through dusk's embrace,
Where every echo finds its place.
The unraveling night reveals the truth,
In silent whispers, forever youth.

Hidden Currents

Beneath the surface, waters churn,
In depth unseen, so much to learn.
Silent streams, they twist and flow,
Carrying dreams where we can't go.

A pulse of life, unseen, profound,
The heartbeats echo, wrap around.
With every wave, a story stirs,
In hidden depths, the silence purrs.

Gentle tides caress the shore,
Secret paths we can explore.
Each ripple whispers, takes its flight,
In currents deep, we find our light.

Mysterious trails that lead us down,
Through water's weave, in night's dark gown.
In hidden currents, truth prevails,
Where silence speaks, and wonder sails.

Let go the shore, embrace the stream,
Find peace within the flowing dream.
For in the depths, our spirits swim,
In currents strong, we learn to brim.

When Whispers Collide

In crowded rooms, the silence hides,
A tapestry where spirit bides.
With every glance, the air ignites,
When whispers collide, hearts take flight.

A gentle brush, the fleeting touch,
An unspoken bond that says so much.
Through fleeting moments, time stands still,
When whispers collide, dreams fulfill.

The world around fades to gray,
In hushed exchanges, come what may.
Subtle secrets in a lover's sigh,
When whispers collide, stars fill the sky.

Eyes locked tight in a dance of fate,
With every beat, our souls relate.
In the quiet, our passions bide,
When whispers collide, we cannot hide.

A shared existence in glances held,
A serenade where silence swelled.
In every heartbeat, stories abide,
When whispers collide, love won't divide.

Harmonies of Old Souls

In ancient woods, the echoes sing,
Of timeless tales and vibrant spring.
Each leaf a note in nature's tune,
In harmonies, we find our rune.

The whispers of the trees awake,
A melody, a fresh heart ache.
With every breeze, the past unfolds,
In harmonies of old souls told.

Together bound by silver threads,
In every word, the spirit spreads.
The laughter blooms, the memories glow,
In harmonies, our shadows grow.

An orchestra of life and time,
In rhythm soft, our hearts align.
With every song, a journey's goal,
In harmonies of old souls whole.

Come walk with me where shadows dwell,
In music sweet, our hearts will swell.
For in these notes, our stories flow,
In harmonies, the ancient know.

Silhouettes of the Past

In shadows cast by fading light,
Memories dance, a ghostly sight.
Whispers echo through the trees,
Time flows like a gentle breeze.

Faded pictures worn and torn,
Stories live where hearts were born.
Fragmented lives in silent sighs,
Hold the truth of ancient ties.

The laughter shared in twilight's glow,
Haunts the nights we used to know.
Each silhouette a tale to tell,
In the heart where shadows dwell.

Through the fog of yesteryears,
We embrace both joy and fears.
In the silence, we find the grace,
Of love that time cannot erase.

Beneath the stars of endless skies,
The echoes of our hearts will rise.
For in the night, the past I see,
A tapestry woven, endlessly.

Sounds of the Void

In the silence, a whisper calls,
Echoes drift through empty halls.
The hush of night, a heavy shroud,
Cradles thoughts that feel so loud.

Footsteps fade like falling leaves,
Leaving traces, memories cleave.
A distant cry of lost intent,
Resonates where time was spent.

The heartbeat of the darkened sky,
Pierces through, a haunting sigh.
Each pulse a story left unheard,
In the silence, dreams are stirred.

From the depths, a rustling sound,
Whispers of the lost abound.
In the void, we seek a way,
To find our voices, night and day.

Yet in the quiet, strength we find,
To weave the threads of soul and mind.
For even voids can resonate,
With secrets time shall not negate.

Threads of Knowing

In gentle winds, the secrets sway,
Woven into life's bright array.
Each thread a link to what we've shared,
A tapestry that fate has dared.

Memories stitched with threads of gold,
Stories waiting to be told.
Fragile fibers hold us tight,
Binding hearts through day and night.

In every knot, a lesson lies,
Through every tear, a chance to rise.
Tangled paths that lead us home,
In every whisper, we are not alone.

Weaving dreams with patient hands,
Crafting futures, shifting sands.
In the loom of life, we find our way,
Connecting moments, come what may.

Each thread, a heartbeat not in vain,
Together, we'll endure the strain.
For through the weave, the truth will show,
In threads of knowing, love will grow.

Tides of Nostalgia

The waves crash softly on the shore,
Whispers of times that were before.
Each sweep a memory, lost and found,
In the dance of the sea, we're bound.

With every ebb, a longing sigh,
The pull of dreams that drift and fly.
Footprints washed by fleeting tides,
In the ocean's heart, a secret hides.

Time flows like water, endlessly,
Carving paths in our memory.
Gold of sunset on the crest,
Reminds us where our hearts find rest.

Tangled in the ocean's song,
We're beckoned where we all belong.
Nostalgia swells within us all,
A gentle tide, a siren's call.

Yet as the moon pulls on our souls,
We dance through life, in sync with goals.
For in the depths, a treasure lies,
In tides of nostalgia, love never dies.

Chants of the Ancient Soul

In whispers soft, the ancients call,
Their voices rise, like shadows tall.
Through time they weave, in silence deep,
Awakening dreams from the eternal sleep.

With every note, the heart ignites,
Echoes dance in the still of nights.
Stories lost in the winds of fate,
An ancient song, we contemplate.

Beneath the stars, wisdom flows,
In every chant, the spirit knows.
They guide our paths through dark and light,
A tapestry spun, both bold and bright.

The earth responds with a gentle sigh,
As we listen, the soul learns to fly.
Every whisper, a sacred thread,
In the silence, the stories spread.

So let us gather, hand in hand,
To the rhythm of the sacred land.
In ancient chants, we find our mold,
Embracing the wisdom of the old.

Footprints in the Sands of Time

In golden grains beneath our feet,
Every step, a tale discreet.
Waves erasing what once has been,
Yet memories linger, soft and keen.

The sun dips low, casting long shades,
Tracing paths where history fades.
With every tide, stories drown,
Yet in our hearts, they wear the crown.

The symbols etched on a fleeting shore,
Remind us all we're so much more.
Foundations built on whispers shared,
In every heart, a journey bared.

Through time we wander, hand in hand,
Embracing moments, building sand.
Each footprint tells of dreams pursued,
In the vastness, souls renewed.

When shadows fall, and twilight gleams,
We chase the echoes of our dreams.
In every grain, a song, a rhyme,
Footprints linger in the sands of time.

Laments of the Unheard

In shadows deep, their voices wane,
Songs of sorrow, etched in pain.
Cries for help, but none to hear,
A silent march through endless fear.

They walk the streets, with heads bowed low,
Carrying burdens, too great to show.
Each tear that falls a silent plea,
In the backdrop of our apathy.

Yet still they rise, with every dawn,
In the quiet, their hope lives on.
For every soul, there lies a dream,
Echoes linger, like a restless stream.

The world may turn and close its eyes,
But in their hearts, the fire flies.
Resilient spirits, bold and proud,
They seek their place within the crowd.

With every sigh, a story weaves,
Laments sung through autumn leaves.
In every heart, the unheard song,
A tapestry where all belong.

Trills in the Twilight

As daylight wanes, the twilight sings,
With trills of joy, the evening brings.
A symphony of colors bright,
Painting dreams in the fading light.

Crickets chirp in a rhythmic hum,
Whispering secrets as night has come.
Stars awaken, one by one,
Filling the sky, our hopes begun.

The breeze carries tales, both old and new,
A lullaby for the hearts that grew.
In every rustle, a soft embrace,
Guiding us to a sacred place.

In twilight's glow, we find our peace,
With gentle whispers that never cease.
Melodies woven in the evening air,
Reminders that beauty lingers there.

So let us dance beneath the skies,
With open hearts and dreaming eyes.
In the twilight, we find our soul,
A symphony where we are whole.

Whispers Through Time

In the quiet night, secrets sigh,
Memories dance under the starlit sky.
Each breeze carries tales from days of yore,
Echoes of laughter, love, and lore.

Leaves rustle softly, a muted tune,
Stars blink above, a wistful boon.
Time slips past, like shadows in flight,
Whispers of ages tangled in light.

Stones bear witness to stories untold,
Of brave hearts and dreams, both timid and bold.
Through the corridors of history's grace,
We find ourselves in a timeless embrace.

Glimmers of hope in the dark we find,
The voice of the past in our heart and mind.
With each gentle sigh of the twilight breeze,
The world remembers, and so too, we seize.

So listen closely, for time has a song,
A melody woven, where we all belong.
In whispers through time, we'll journey and roam,
Finding our place, in the grand tapestry—home.

Shadows of the Unseen

Shadows linger where light cannot tread,
Whispers of silence, stories unsaid.
In corners forgotten, they patiently wait,
Guardians of secrets, shaping our fate.

Figures entwined in the twilight glow,
Dancing on edges where few dare to go.
Veils of the past weave designs in the night,
Shadows unveil what hides from the light.

The moon holds its breath, watching in awe,
As dreams intertwine with fate's gentle law.
In the stillness, wisdom takes flight,
Truths come alive in the absence of light.

Silent companions, they guide and they tease,
Inviting us deep into thought's quiet trees.
To understand more of what lies concealed,
In shadows of the unseen, our hearts are revealed.

Eclipsed by the mundane, we often miss,
The beauty found in the fleeting abyss.
But if we embrace what the shadows bestow,
In their gentle embrace, our spirits will grow.

Reflections in Still Waters

Calm waters shimmer beneath the pale moon,
Mirrors of midnight, serene and immune.
With each gentle ripple, dreams start to rise,
Reflections of truth hidden deep in our eyes.

The cool night's embrace wraps tight like a shawl,
Echos of whispers, as shadows enthrall.
Each wave tells a story, a memory's grace,
In still waters deep, we find our own space.

Stars dapple skies, eternal yet near,
Guiding our hearts to release all our fear.
Through moments of silence, we come to see,
Reflections of soul, in the vastness, we're free.

Gentle like breezes that stroke the still glass,
Thoughts drift like clouds, effortlessly pass.
In the quietness, wisdom begins,
A chance for renewal, where stillness begins.

So pause by the water, let go and let flow,
Life's most profound answers, reflect what we know.
In still waters lying, may we find below,
The depths of our being, where true waters flow.

Resonance of Forgotten Dreams

In the echoes of night, memories hum,
Whispers of hopes that once were, now numb.
Lost in the silence, they seek to be heard,
The resonance soft, like a long-forgotten word.

Dusty old pages turn gently in time,
Each line sings a verse, a lost paradigm.
Faded ambitions linger, ask for a chance,
In shadows of dreams, we rediscover romance.

Beneath the surface of everyday strife,
Lies the heart's longing, the pulse of life.
Listening closely, we tune in our schemes,
Awakening voices of our faded dreams.

Like starlight that glimmers on dark, empty nights,
Fading yet vibrant, they spark our delights.
Resonance echoes through chambers of heart,
Reminding us gently from which we won't part.

So treasure those wishes once whispered at night,
In their soft melancholy, there lies hidden light.
For the resonance of dreams, though tired they seem,
Can still guide our spirits to where we redeem.